Originally Published under licence 3 October 2011 by Searching Finance Ltd, 8 Whitehall Road, London
W7 2JE, UK

ISBN-13: 978-0615598611 (TLG Press)

Typeset and designed by Deirdré Gyenes

Google Wallet and the New Retail Ecosystem

By David W. Schropfer

About the author

David W. Schropfer is an international business leader with two decades of management experience ranging from telecommunications to payment systems. Mr. Schropfer is a Partner with the internationally recognized consulting firm, The Luciano Group, where he leads its Mobile Payment and Mobile Commerce practice. Earlier in his career, he was Senior Vice President with IDT Telecom, and a Business Development Officer for Capital One. He has served on the Board of Directors for multiple companies, and is a frequent speaker at industry conferences and trade shows. After graduating Boston College, David earned an Executive MBA from the University of Miami.

About the Luciano Group

The Luciano Group provides executives in the global telecommunications industry with management and operational consulting services. We are the leading provider of strategic and tactical programs that create new sources of revenue, increased profits, and improved operational efficiency and performance for our clients. http://lucianogp.com/

About Searching Finance

Searching Finance Ltd is a dynamic new voice in knowledge provision for the financial services and related professional sectors. Our mission is to provide expert, highly relevant and actionable information and analysis. For more information, please visit www.searchingfinance.com

Contents

Table of Figures

Executive summary

The Mobile Payments industry is starting over. When the Google Wallet launched in September 20, 2011, the first test of a remarkable new financial ecosystem began. But despite the apparent success of traditional mobile payments products like M-PESA in Kenya and South Africa, Google and rival Isis have decided to rewrite the business model – and for good reason. Actually, four good reasons:

1. Significant revenue is available from the advertising, retention and rewards programs, leaving the usual payments fees to the payments companies.

2. The payments ecosystem cannot afford new categories. The existing players are companies with considerable resources and the willingness to use their resources to thwart a new category of entrants.

3. Regulatory changes are pressuring known revenue streams, increasing the motivation for existing players in the payments ecosystem to protect position.

4. Cash is resilient to other tender types in developed worlds, not so in developing countries.

As a result, both Isis and the Google Wallet products are creating a simple strategy which lets the payment ecosystem continue to charge and earn as much as possible from the payments business. The new revenue these companies seek to earn comes from two vulnerable industries: advertising and loyalty. Google, with its extreme interest in data collection and distribution, will likely seek new revenue from that channel also.

The strategies of these two companies, which are likely to be eventually joined by Apple and Amazon in their approach, has substantially slowed mobile commerce development in the rest of the developed world. Even Japan, which has used an NFC-like technology for most of the last decade, is highly interested in understanding the results of the American experiments before committing to a long-term strategy.

The new revenue these companies seek to earn comes from two vulnerable industries: advertising and loyalty.

And they are not in a hurry. The only short-range communication standard with approval from the International Standards Organization is ISO/IEC

14443, known simply as Near-Field Communications or NFC. To use either the Google Wallet or Isis product as they are currently understood, the customer will either need a phone with an NFC chip built in (which is in exactly one model out of hundreds of models of mobile phones in the US – The Samsung Nexus S) and merchants will need to invest in NFC readers at their cash registers (also known as POS terminals).

Whether the US experiments succeed or fail, one thing is certain – the unenhanced peer-to-peer payments systems like M-PESA have no chance to reach the mainstream of the US or any developed country. The environment is simply too hostile from entrenched payments incumbents, and from feature-rich new services.

A different breed of service that includes advertising and rewards programs as well as data services will vastly overshadow stand-alone mobile payments products

A different breed of service that includes advertising and rewards programs as well as data services will vastly overshadow stand-alone mobile payments products. These new services are called "mobile commerce."

Summary of mobile commerce

Jim Stapleton, chief sales officer of Isis, recently was quoted as follows:

Figure 1: Quote from Jim Stapleton, Head of Sales and Account Management, Isis

"The *industry* is poised to fundamentally **modernize** the **payment** experience and **enhance** the way that **consumers**, **merchants** and **banks** interact."

The industry to which Mr. Stapleton referred – mobile commerce – does not exist as a functioning or mature industry. The form, function, features, benefits, roles, and players that will exist in the new mobile commerce industry have yet to be decided. The activity and momentum is already of such a high volume, the partnerships have already been formed and broken, businesses have already been launched and closed, and several business models have already been dismissed as ineffective. Of course, these decisions are being made without the benefit of test results on statistically significant portions of the population of first world nations. With only Japan as a guide of what to do and what not to do, the rest of the world is quickly attempting to extrapolate lessons learned from DoCoMo and other Japanese mobile commerce providers, while analyzing and revisiting data from the known market of payments, loyalty, mobile, and consumer retention- which have existed in Europe and America for multiple years.

In addition, Mr. Stapleton's use of the term "modernization" implies a dramatic change in the features, benefits, and operational structure of payments. Whatever the interpretation, it is clear that Mr. Stapleton believes that the wallet format is the most likely industry to succeed the payments industry, as it exists today.

The research and analysis presented in this report reaches the same conclusion: the wallet format will prevail as the industry standard of mobile commerce.

Early consolidation

Approximately 60 new companies, with various roles in the overall mobile commerce ecosystem, have emerged over the last 12 to 36 months. The mobile network operators, on the other hand, have formed joint ventures in Canada, the United States, and the United Kingdom. In the United States, the joint venture (Isis) has illustrated its general concept, features, and value-add to merchants and consumers, but specific details have yet to be revealed, leaving significant doubt about the position and their ability to come to market. In parallel, the payments industry is moving quickly and investing heavily to ensure that the mobile commerce systems of tomorrow will utilize the established networks and communication channels that these businesses have built over the last 50 years.

The available models in the mobile commerce ecosystem currently emerging in the United States, Canada, and the United Kingdom are consolidating quickly. Some of these start-up companies have closed their doors for good, and others have "suspended operations" in hopes of reorganizing (like Bling Nation). Some companies have embraced the concepts of biometrics (like FaceCash) while others focus squarely on loyalty programs and value incentives.

The winning combination

The Google Wallet, and its future competitors, are leveraging a set of technology changes, namely:

- JACC (Just Another Connected Computer);
- NFC (Near-Field Communication);
- EMV (Europay, MasterCard, Visa, a global standard for inter-operation of integrated circuit cards);
- TSM (Trusted Services Manager, a provisioning role); and
- Smart phone operating systems.

In addition, the Google Wallet and its competitors may target a combination of several different elements of older business models:

- Prepaid Cards (also known as stored value cards);
- Processing fees;
- Loyalty/rewards account management fees;
- Data mining;
- Breakage;
- Advertising and conversion.

The overriding conclusion is that emerging mobile wallet companies have a significant value proposition to offer to both merchants and consumers with little or no new fees. In fact, the data reported in this analysis suggests that mobile wallets may ultimately <u>reduce</u> the total cost of marketing and sales for merchants.

Mobile wallet services and products are likely to cost merchants less money than traditional advertising campaigns because mobile wallet companies will have revenue from several existing sources that remove the need to pass along new charges to manufactures – a time-tested model for merchants.

For consumers, the cost of these products will likely remain free, depending on the reload payment type (see Chapter 5), and the convenience could be remarkable because of the auto-link to loyalty programs and easy access to other forms of discounts.

And these mobile products and services will look beyond the traditional payment network for revenue (see Chapter 1). Maintaining the overwhelmingly strong brand value of payment products such as Visa and MasterCard, and the substantial infrastructure of processors and financial institutions does not need to be bypassed or rebuilt to enable these mobile wallet efficiencies.

Finally, most mobile wallet products will be more secure than magnetic stripe credit cards based on new technology and standards such as EMV and TSM (see Chapters 2 and 4).

All of the elements are in place for extreme disruption in the payment, loyalty, and advertising industries. Creative uses of new technology, effective uses of the thinking power of mobile devices, and revenue streams from unlikely sources make the mobile wallet model, and its service providers formidable competitors that will emerge over the next three years.

Chapter 1

The current payments industry

1.1 Review of payments industry

A return to the four party systems is not likely as a result of mobile payments. However, it is important to revisit the notion that automated payments is the act of moving funds from one account to the other in exchange for goods or services that a consumer acquires from a merchant.

In the late 1960s when Bank of America first issued its BankAmerica card, the idea was to "settle" with the bank that held the account for the merchant, and distribute the funds in a lump sum to each other bank. Of course, the reality of the system has grown extensively over the last 50 years, leading to the more complex system in the chart below:

Figure 2: Payment

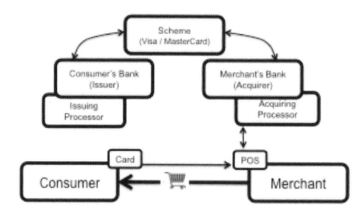

During the last decade, the payment system has nearly doubled its penetration in the United States payments market. In 2002, general-purpose cards represented 35.4% of transaction dollar volumes, with checks accounting for 41.9%. General-purpose cards overtook checks in dollar volume for the first time in 2004, with the penetration of checks sinking to 32.1% while general-purpose cards jumped to 47%. Then, in 2008, checks fell below cash for the first time at 24.2% with cash at 24.6%. In that same year, general-purpose cards exceeded 51.1%, the only category ever to exceed half of the overall transaction volume. By 2012, general-purpose cards are expected to reach almost 64% with checks plummeting down to 10.4%. Interestingly, cash has maintained a steady market share over these years. The low point of cash in terms of market penetration occurred in 2002 at 22.7% and the high point is expected to be 26% in 2012.

1.2 Payments penetration in the US

Figure 3: US market penetration of general-purpose cards, 2002 to 2012

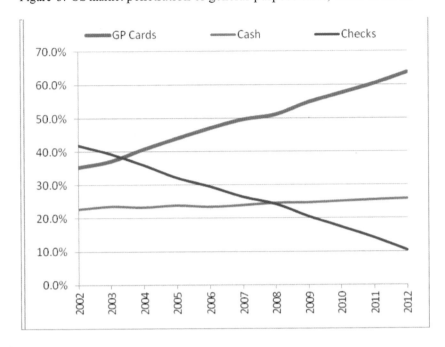

Sources: Aite Group, Nilson Report, author calculations

Mobile commerce will not replace general-purpose cards or checks necessarily. Instead, general-purpose cards are likely to become available through mobile payments and mobile commerce and mobile wallet systems. For clarity, a transaction settled through general-purpose card using the mobile wallet as a conduit will effectively use the same processors, the same methods, and the same payments industry process that would be employed today to settle a transaction using a typical credit card or debit card.

Mobile commerce will not replace general-purpose cards or checks necessarily

1.3 Mobile Network Operator billing

Just as we saw with the rise of PayPal in the early part of the last decade to present, settlement through mobile network operators (MNOs) continues to be significantly higher in cost than settlement through any of the payment types listed above, in some cases up to 500% higher. Without a dramatic change in the prices that MNOs charged to merchants for the purpose of settling transactions, it is unlikely that MNO penetration will achieve significant penetration in the payments market.

1.4 No room for competition

The new Google Wallet product includes separate features and benefits previously included in three disparate industries: advertising, loyalty and retention, and payments. This application does not simply improve the customer shopping experience: it fundamentally alters it, providing information and decision tools unlike anything a customer has previously experienced. The business model of the product is different; the partner bank (Citi) appears to be making the same money it has always made through interchange, which is essentially a fee charged to a merchant for accepting a credit card.

The combination of new services, new technology, old industries, and new ideas engendered in the Google Wallet and Isis will make the environment difficult to other entrants. AMEX and Visa have also announced products that appear to be similar to the Google Wallet. PayPal opened an actual retail location in New York City to demonstrate to merchants the shopping experience of consumers based on PayPal's product. Also, Amazon is rumoured to be working on similar services as well. The Google Wallet, the Isis product, the Visa digital wallet – all share a common set of features and benefits to both a retailer and consumer, despite the fact that none of these product have made it to the market or even a market test. All of these products have new business models that rely on a combination of revenue streams from different industries. An analysis of these revenue streams, and their potential, is critical to understanding these new products and the profit they will bring to the competitors.

1.5 Rewards and loyalty systems

In addition to the payment players and businesses organized to settle funds between consumer accounts and merchant accounts, there exist two ancillary businesses often connected to the processors on the acquiring and issuing side of the payment process: these are the rewards or loyalty systems.

While these systems tend to be interchangeable in name, rewards and loyalty programs are designed to change consumer behaviour. For the purpose of this discussion, a rewards program is a system attached to an issuing processor designed to incite usage of a specific consumer general-purpose card. These programs have included points programs, free merchandise, cash-back, and other incentives designed to continuously motivate the consumer to reach
for a specific card in their wallet, assuming the customer has more than one. Conveniently, these programs tend to be automatic, with the consumer needing to do no other activity than purchase goods to accumulate virtual currency or other rewards promised as part of the program. However, redemption of these programs tends to be a manual process, and many of the points are never redeemed. In a mobile commerce environment, both of these processes are likely to be completely automated.

Loyalty programs and systems generally refer to programs intended to bring a consumer into a specific merchant with incentives such as coupons, discounts, and other incentives.

Figure 4: The rewards and loyalty accounts in the US

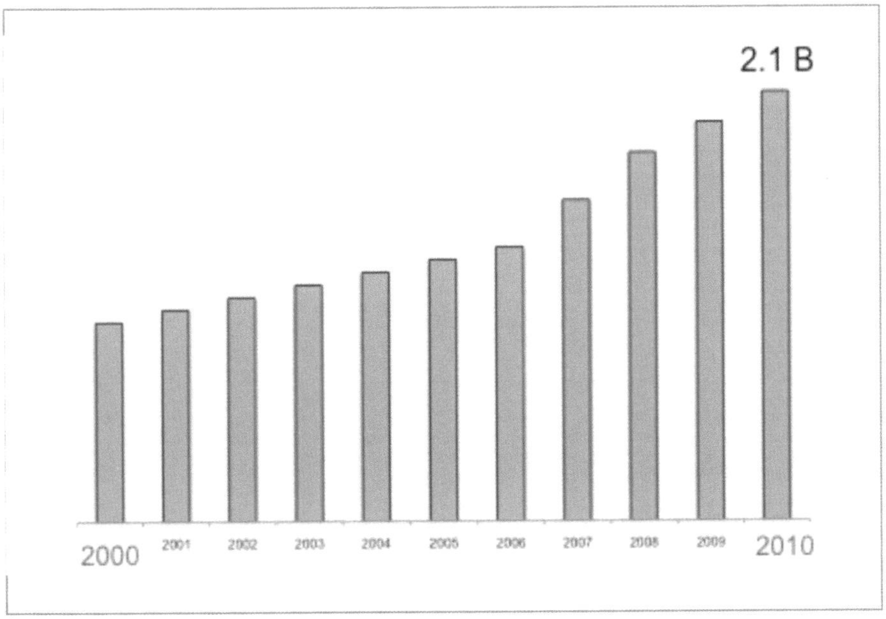

Source: Colloquy

Remarkably, there are over 2.1 billion loyalty and rewards programs currently issued to customers in the United States. With only 300 million total population, this equates to almost seven accounts for every individual in the United States. While this is an overwhelming number of accounts, it is indicative of the success of these programs overall. However, it is unclear how many of these accounts remain active or inactive at any given point in time. In addition, these programs can be confusing to consumers because they don't know which program necessarily provides the best incentive for each purchase made by each consumer.

In a mobile commerce environment, the entire architecture depicted in Figure 2, inclusive of the reward systems and loyalty programs, plus all acquirers, issuers and processors, plus the schemes, are all part of a system that will be challenged by the mobile wallet. Although it may seem counter-intuitive that the mobile wallet will rely on payment cards to process most of its transactions, and any payment card will continue to use the system in Figure 2, it is the subtle differences of the mobile wallet that we will explore in the next sections which could gradually erode and isolate the system.

The entire payments architecture ... will be challenged by the mobile wallet

1.6 Merchant tolerance

Understanding the accounting practices of retailers and merchants is a significant factor when reviewing how merchants book the costs of these various programs, and how much they're willing to spend.

In a study by international consultancy Deloitte, the company estimated that merchants are willing to pay between 7% and 9% of a transaction amount to acquire a new sale. This figure is blended across multiple lines of business, given that some merchandise has a retail margin of 300% (such as cosmetics) while others have an extremely low margin of around 10% (electronics).

Figure 5: Merchants Tolerance for Cost of Sale

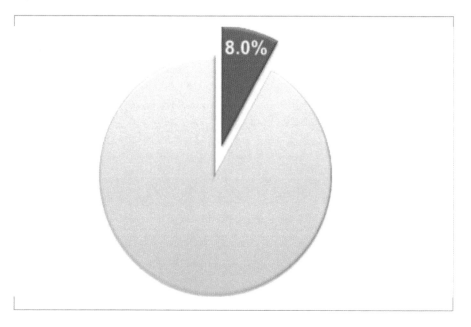

Rewards programs, loyalty programs, and advertising are generally accounted for within the merchant tolerance of 7% to 9%. When managing a budget for these programs, merchants will attempt to fit their expenditure on these various types of programs within roughly 8%. It is important to note that loyalty and rewards programs at point of sale reached meaningful volume only in the last two decades. Prior to that, this entire 7% to 9% of sales was allocated solely to traditional advertising media such as magazines, newspapers, television, and radio. Today, that advertising spend is under additional attack from alternate media such as social media, the Internet, and other electronic forms that did not exist 20 years ago.

Merchants may use 'Co-Op' advertising to recoup mobile wallet investments from manufacturers

Many of the larger retailers leverage the practice of billing manufacturers for advertising their products. The logic is that paid media exposure of a specific product has value to the company that manufactures that product. For example, a newspaper advertisement that promotes the logo of Best Buy will be paid entirely by Best Buy. However, a newspaper advertisement that features a Sony Television that is on sale at Best Buy will be paid – in part – by Sony. This technique is called 'cooperative advertising' (or simply "co-op"), and will likely be used in mobile wallet scenarios where merchants invest in technology (such as NFC Posters and 'check-in' stations), partnerships (such as Google Wallet and Isis), and new promotional methods. Most of these merchant investments support and promote the products supplied by manufacturers, and the accepted model of cooperative advertising suggests that merchants can – and will – pass along some of their mobile wallet investment costs to product manufactures.

While it is not possible to prove the future of the advertising industry, or merchant tolerance to pay for these programs, one of the key hypotheses of this report is that the advertising space will continue to come under attack both from new, more effective forms of media (in this case mobile commerce) as well as a new concept of including payments as a form of cost of sales instead of G&A (general and administrative expense).

One prevalent ideas is to absorb payment processing within the new media advertising concepts supported only by mobile phones

My grandfather, Frank Schropfer, was a brilliant businessman and a skilled accountant before he died in 2006. In my youth, my grandfather taught me some basics of accounting. At the time, I believed that accounting was less interesting than watching grass grow. Studying the topic many years later during my MBA course studies removed all doubt. However, when considering the opportunity of mobile commerce to penetrate the payment system, loyalty programs, and advertising programs, it is important to consider how merchants account for these different programs.

Payment systems are accounted not as cost of sales, but rather as G&A. Unlike cost of sales, which support a tolerance of 7–9%, most businesses (including retailers) seek to constantly minimize G&A. In other words, wherever an opportunity exists to lower the cost of accepting credit and debit cards and other payment types, a retailer will always seek to do that.

Later in this report, this becomes important when we look at various emerging models available through mobile commerce because one of the prevalent ideas is to absorb payments processing within the new media advertising concepts supported only by mobile phones.

1.7 Conclusion of current system

For convenience, we will refer to the combined payments, loyalty, and rewards systems using the one macro term: "payments system". As we have described in this section, the payments system enjoys significant market share, steady growth, highly mature processes and standards, and specialized vendors and providers that have all perfected their operations over the course of the last several decades. Although the payments system may not be perfect, it works reliably, securely and predictably. Over the years and decades to come, this system may be restructured, repositioned, or even dismantled in lieu of a new system. However, for at least ten and perhaps twenty more years, the payments system will be used to settle payments between merchants and customers. So the question is not whether or not the payments system will go away soon (it won't). The right question is market share: will mobile wallets maintain support the payments system, or will mobile wallets begin to exploit the vulnerabilities to the payment system.

Chapter 2

Vulnerability of the current payments system

2.1 Three areas of vulnerability

Like other industries, the current payment system is vulnerable in three general areas:

- Technology changes;
- Changes in market conditions; and
- Regulatory pressures.

Technology changes include both the equipment and operating systems. In the case of mobile commerce, equipment technology that is changing the payments system includes: SIM card technology, smart phone technology, smart phone operating systems, applications (apps) for smart phone operating systems, micro-SD cards, NFC, TSM, EMV and other items. Regarding communication systems and operating systems, the changes that will impact the availability of mobile commerce include advances in GSM technology (2.5G, 3G, 4GLTE, 4G Wi-Fi, CDMA, and other technologies).

Changes in market conditions refer to a combination of new business models and new market entrants. Regarding market conditions, the technology changes that will impact the payments industry, specifically a mobile phone that can support its own operating system (aka the smart phone) will become a new "form factor" to a typical plastic card such as a debit card or credit card. In short, the ability of a smart phone to present multiple payment types in a single view to the user will enable new ways of presenting choices to the consumer, and new methods of inciting the consumer to choose one payment type over another. This is called "tender steering" and will be discussed in later chapters of this report. Regarding new market entrants, this refers to companies that previously did not participate in the payment system, such as Google, Apple, Amazon.com, and all mobile network operators.

Regulatory pressures include all changes in the regulatory requirements of the government, and self-imposed standards within the industry.

2.2 Case study: Telecommunications and payments industries development compared

Over the last 30 years, the telecommunications industry represents one example of a business that experienced severe declines in its average revenue per unit (ARPU) due to regulatory forces, market conditions, and new technology.

Figure 7: Case study of long-distance decline in ARPU

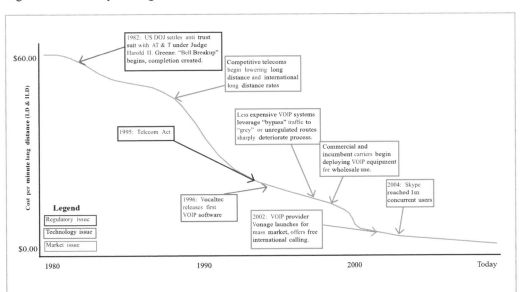

Source: US Federal Communications Commissions (FCC), Telegeography, author calculations and industry analysis

Notice the relevant turning points in the case study above share several historical points with the payment system:

Telecommunications (long-distance)	Corollary to payment systems
1. Complaints about monopoly: Significant concern began in the 1960s and 1970s regarding the lack of price competition in the United States telecommunications market. At the time, one company – AT&T – held the sole license for all Mexican international telecommunications activity. All complaints centered on the concept that without competition, the cost of service was artificially inflated. In the early 1980s, the average cost of a long-distance call, including international calls, was $60 per minute. Today, that figure varies between "free" and mere pennies per minute for almost every location on earth. Let's review how that happened. In 1982, the United States Department of Justice settled a lawsuit with AT&T under Judge Harold H Greene. The settlement became known as the "Bell breakup" as the telecommunications monopoly of the United States was eliminated, and multiple new companies known as Regional Bell Operating Systems (RBOCs) were formed.	**Complaints about banks and payment systems:** Since the 1970s, retailers have had relatively few choices in systems providers for payment types other than cash and checks. While cashing checks were directly deposited by the retailer into the retailer's bank account at no additional cost to the merchant, accepting a credit card or (later) a debit card presented significant charges to the merchant ranging from 1.5% to 5%, or higher. In other words, if a retailer accepted a credit card as payment for $100-worth of merchandise, the retailer would only receive between $95 and $98.50 when the transaction was deposited into its bank account. Consumers, however, did not generally complain about these services because the cost of accepting credit and debit cards did not directly impact them (in other words, for $100-worth of merchandise, a consumer paid $100). Banks and the payment industry argued that the combination of security, privacy, accuracy, and speed of settlement within its electronic payment systems was a costly endeavor, one that deserved to be compensated. In addition, one of the primary arguments of the payment industry began with the advent of credit cards and stemmed from the concept that extending credit presented risk on the part of the issuer of the credit (in most cases, banks) and that assumption of risk also deserved to be compensated. All these issues combined as Walmart and Sears filed suit against Visa and MasterCard on 1996, and was settled until 2003. According to the New York Times, Visa paid approximately $2 billion to retailers and reduced the fees it charged merchants on some debit card purchases. MasterCard agreed to pay $1 billion, and (like Visa) also agreed to cut its fees.
2. New market entrants: In the 1980s and early 1990s, the RBOCs were permitted to compete with each other on matters such as long-distance and international long-distance, and immediate price erosion began.	In 1998, a company called PayPal launched a new service originally designed to let people send money to each other using a new, low-cost payment system. The fundamental difference between the PayPal scheme and the traditional payment system scheme is that PayPal was not a bank – instead it acted more like a macro database provider. This is the first large-scale occurrence of a "virtual currency". For example, when $5 was paid from one PayPal account to another PayPal account, PayPal's sole responsibility was to debit the value of one account and credit the other for the same amount. Notably, no funds are moved in this transaction. In fact, funds are not transmitted from one institution to another until a customer transfers funds from a traditional bank account into a PayPal account, or vice versa. When PayPal receives these funds, however, PayPal simply deposit the funds in a bank account contracted by PayPal, and is then responsible for managing the virtual currency in each individual account. This difference to its operational process enabled PayPal to avoid becoming a registered bank in the United States, although later PayPal would have to register as a bank in the European Union. Fundamentally, PayPal's operational systems were more efficient and less expensive than the payments network with the cost approaching zero dollars for each incremental transaction because the single PayPal service can attach to any bank or payment device. But PayPal was limited to operating on the Internet only, and brick-and-mortar transactions would not be within reach until the advent of mobile commerce in 2011, when PayPal first became available at Starbucks through a reloadable mobile commerce product.

3. Regulatory changes: in 1996, the United States passed the Telecom Act to permanently open the door to competition from a variety of different providers, both inside and outside of the United States. International long-distance providers were able to acquire a "214 license" which legally allowed a company to send telecommunications voice and data traffic from the United States to other parts the world.	In May 2009, the United States Congress passed the Credit Card Responsibility And Disclosure (CARD) Act, which would be implemented in three phases over the next two years. Phase 1 of the card act focused on ensuring that the payments industry provided better notification to its consumers, enacting a 45-day notice before any changes in the annual percentage rate of most credit card products, and ensuring that invoices were mailed at least 21 days before the due date to avoid systematic late payments from consumers and the associated fees with these late payments. Phase 2 of CARD Act went farther, effectively limiting increases to the annual percentage rates of many credit card products, while also limiting delinquency penalties for card products. Phase 3 of CARD Act further limited fees and also limited multiplying penalties on most credit cards. In addition, the Dodd-Frank Wall Street Reform Act passed the United States Congress in 2010, and was signed into law the president Barack Obama on July 21, 2010. Sen. Durbin (Democrat: Illinois) proposes an amendment to the Dodd-Frank Act, which, among other things, limits interchange fees on debit cards from major banks to approximately $0.21 per transaction plus 0.05% (5 basis points) – a significant decrease from the 1.5% to 3% interchange fees traditionally charged for the service. Attempts to delay the implementation of the Durbin amendment failed on June 9, 2011. And, as of the writing of this report, this amendment is set to go into effect in October 2011.
4. Voice over Internet Protocol – VoIP – was a technology originally developed in the early 1990s. The technology was remarkably different from the traditional telecommunications compression protocol called Time Division Multiplexing in three important ways: (1) it uses the same Internet protocol used by every Internet website, and any content delivered through the Internet; and (2) the equipment utilized for this purpose was significantly less expensive than TDM. But most importantly, the network itself was remarkably less expensive to use than traditional "private line" networks. To gain access to the "Internet" network, an individual or a company really needs to contract with an Internet Service Provider, or ISP. The price for bandwidth on the Internet was routinely about 1/10 the cost for the same bandwidth on a private line network. The combination of less expensive equipment and significantly less expensive network costs made VoIP a game changer in the telecom industry. In 1995, a company called VocalTec released its first VoIP software for mass adoption, and seven years later a company called Vonage launched its VoIP service to the general public in United States.	The payments system will be affected by an assortment of technology changes, which will produce efficiency, speed, and cost reduction. The mobile phone technologies include: SIM card technology, smart phone technology, smart phone operating systems, applications (apps) for smart phone operating systems, micro-SD cards, near field communication (NFC). New services and protocols that leverage the mobile phone as a conduit will include elements of trusted service management (TSM), Europay-MasterCard-Visa (EMV), and other items. Over-the-air (OTA) communications network changes include which will impact the availability of mobile commerce include GSM technology (2.5 G, 3G, 4GLTE, 4G Wi-Fi, CDMA, and other technologies). In addition, the inexpensive networks connected to both typical POS devices at retail stores, plus the inexpensive networks connected to mobile phones and smart phones combined to provide real-time updates of loyalty programs, rewards programs and the like for consumer benefit. Finally, the computing power of a smart phone allows the device to act like a computer and arithmetically calculate the best combination of payment products and loyalty products for any given purchase at any given reseller. These advancements are unprecedented in the payments and loyalty industries.

Chapter 3

Elements of mobile commerce

3.1 Three elements of mobile commerce

Mobile commerce embodies elements of advances in technology, and changes in industry competitors and business models, as described in the previous chapter.

Mobile commerce focuses on three different elements:

- Customer acquisition;
- Conversion; and
- Transaction.

Figure 8: The elements of mobile commerce

3.2 Customer acquisition

Typically the advertising industry is the source of newly acquired customers in the marketplace. Mobile commerce allows for other types of businesses that can inform a consumer of discounts, and other offers that are geographically located near where the customer is located at any given point in time; many of these services are called location-based services, or LBS.

3.3 Conversion

In the retail industry, the term "conversion" generally means changing a customer from a person browsing through your store to a person buying at your store. This area is converted from a variety of different tactics and techniques, many of which are supported by the smart phone and mobile commerce, namely: loyalty programs which reward customers for repeat purchase behaviour, retention programs which prevent customers from taking their business to a competitor, in-store sales and promotions – the oldest form of conversion technique (in other words, inform your customer about a sale price or discount price or a low-priced item that the customer was not aware of prior to entering the store). All of these techniques, and many more, are illustrated in Figure 8, and will be available widely through mobile commerce practices of the future.

3.4 Transactions

This is the process typically owned by the payments industry. Rewards programs and other incentives offered by banks are all designed to keep a particular product "top of wallet", meaning that you as a consumer are more likely to use a particular payment type over another payment type in your everyday purchases. In a mobile commerce environment, however, all this changes because all of the payment types available through your mobile phone are presented in such a way that the user is indifferent about which product he or she chooses. Beyond that, a technology called "tender steering" (which allows a retailer to provide incentives to customers to use a particular type of card to pay) could even rank the payment types based on a number of tag-related factors, such as a real-time incentive discount or other factors.

3.5 Current state of mobile commerce

3.5.1 Japan and Korea

To analyse mobile commerce ecosystems in the first world, a review of Japan and Korea is necessary because of the media attention these markets have received in the new mobile payment space over the last several years. Unfortunately, systems notably lack integration with loyalty programs, seamless application of points and other virtual currencies during a purchase, and any element of tender steering. While services available in Japan and Korea are convenient, mature, and heavily utilized, they appear to have not ventured beyond the two categories of (a) remittance; and (b) information.

While services available in Japan and Korea are convenient, mature, and heavily utilized, they appear to have not ventured beyond the two categories of (a) remittance; and (b) information

3.5.2 Remittance

As early as 2002 and 2003, Japanese consumers were able to use the web browser on their smart phones to access websites that had merchandise, services, and other content available for purchase. Similar to a typical online transaction from a desktop computer, this approach required that the customer enter their credit card number onto the website through the interface of their smart phone web browser.

In 2004, NTT DoCoMo, Japan's largest mobile network operator, began selling smart phone handsets which used an interesting chip called FeliCa, which made it possible for a smart phone to both encrypt and communicate multiple forms of secure data, including bank account numbers, credit card numbers, account balances, personal identification, and other elements. The FeliCa chip communicates through a form of a radio wave to a nearby electronic cash register or vending machine, (similar to NFC), enabling the smart phone user to make a purchase using only their smart phone and an existing cash or credit account.

Essentially, consumers can download an application for the multitude of payment options that exist in Japan today, including accounts that do not require the customer to have a bank account (similar to both M-PESA in Kenya and T-Cash in Haiti), traditional credit cards, traditional bank cards, and other products. In Japan, a credit card issuer is not necessarily a financial institution. Most major retailers and manufacturing companies issue credit cards that can only be used for purchases of their products, and in some cases these accounts are never issued on a card at all – the account itself exists only on the smart phone.

There are 127 million men, women and children in Japan, and over 28 million registered mobile payments accounts. It could be years before the US and Europe catch-up to Japan's penetration of these smart phone wallet services.

Neither Japan nor the similar Korean markets seem to have proven mobile commerce ecosystem, although their penetration of mobile payments systems is undeniable. It is important to understand the definition of ecosystem to appreciate why this is the case.

3.5.3 Information

In both markets, the mobile phone could also be used as an information-gathering device. Available only to smart phones which had an embedded camera, consumers could use apps specifically written to use the camera to "scan" 2-D and 3-D barcodes on products, posters, even the paper liner of a McDonald's plastic tray. Also, "smart posters" were invented in Japan. These items were literally paper or cardboard posters that had a FeliCa chip with a tiny script of information included in the poster. The user would merely need to tap their phone in the specified place to communicate with the information on the poster, which typically activated another application on the smart phone to produce the intended image or information set to the customer on their smart phone.

While the connection to information through either barcodes or FeliCa provided a feature-rich experience for consumers, these programs typically were not integrated with the payment experience or loyalty programs.

Chapter 4

Market changes enabling mobile commerce

4.1 NFC – Near-Field Communications

NFC is just another two-way radio signal that allows one device to communicate with another device. Your smart phone already emits more than one kind of two-way signal, including (in most cases) Bluetooth and Wi-Fi. So, it may seem unnecessary to have another two-way signal coming from your smart phone.

However, the significant advantage of NFC is the range.

Figure 9: Capability of NFC-enabled smartphone compared to EMV card and magnetic stripe

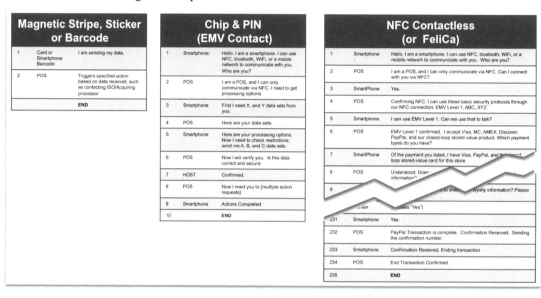

Both Bluetooth and Wi-Fi are signals that your enabled smart phone can connect with from around 10 to 50 feet away, and even more in some cases. When conducting a retail transaction with your phone, you probably don't want your communication signal to carry that far, in case you initiate a transaction without knowing about it by accidentally pressing a button or two on your smart phone when you are in the proximity of an electronic cash register.

If you use NFC as the communication channel between your smart phone and the electronic cash register, the range is not a problem because the NFC range is approximately 10 centimeters. Your smart phone virtually needs to be in contact with the device it is communicating with, which is exactly the point – no unintentional communication.

NFC is most likely to become the standard of choice in securing the communication stream between a smart phone and a cash register

NFC is most likely to become the standard of choice in securing the communication stream between a smart phone and a cash register. Although NFC takes many forms, and exists from many different companies today, they generally take the form of a sticker, or an add-on device, or embedded in the form of an electronic component into the smart phone itself by the manufacturer.

4.2 JACC - Just Another Connected Computer

Consider that the mobile phone is 'just another connected computer' (JACC) because it can connect to the Internet at any time via the mobile network, Wi-Fi, etc. Also, a retail POS device is also a kind of JACC because it is connected via an IP address. NFC allows these two connected computers to communicate back and forth with ease.

NFC essentially connects two computers together (in this case, a customer's smart phone and a retailer's POS device), allowing each computer to ask questions, and allowing the other to answer. Obviously, the Internet allows exactly the same thing, except that the Internet is not inherently wireless, like NFC.

Figure 10: Brick-and-mortar sales volume versus Internet retailing

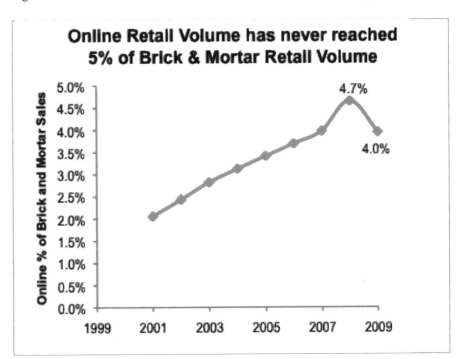

Source: US Dept of Commerce, Nilson Report, author calculations

Consider the only predicate existing in the marketplace for connecting to fully functional computers together for the purpose of retail purchases. The reference here is obviously the Internet. Internet shopping, or online retailing, began in earnest in the late 1990s. By the year 2000, online retailing had achieved approximately 2% of the purchase volume of all brick-and-mortar transactions (meaning all transactions completed at a physical retail store, as shown in Figure 10. On the surface, this may seem to indicate that connecting two computers does not materially change the consumer experience because online retailing never surpasses the 5% mark versus brick-and-mortar retailers. However, this conclusion is incorrect.

Since the beginning of commerce, transactions required face-to-face contact. The modern embodiment is the retail store, where a customer physically enters a building or other area in which merchandise or services are offered, and a customer purchases these items. While Internet retailing may have presented new conveniences, economies, and experiences for the consumer, the bricks-and-mortar experience is impossible to replace. Internet retailing has illustrated the retail industry could be eroded somewhat, but it could not be replaced. However, the 4.7% penetration that online retailing achieved in 2008 is significant, considering that the overall market was approximately $5.5 trillion that year, so 4.7% represented a remarkable dollar value.

4.3 TSM – Trusted Service Management

All these technologies come together to form a significantly more secure payment environment using mobile commerce, such as the Google Wallet or Isis, then any plastic card

Did you own a mobile phone in the late 1980s? Did you hear about friends or colleagues who had the experience of opening their mobile phone bill only to find hundreds of dollars of charges and phone calls that they never made? Also, have you experienced, or have you known anybody who has experienced, any of these issues in the last 15 years? This is called mobile cloning, and it cost consumers and mobile network operators multiple millions of dollars in the early years of mobile telephone services.

The solution was a new security technology, which solved the problem. For simplicity, the solution included putting a set of credentials – your secrets – on the SIM card of a mobile phone. Whenever you make a phone call on your mobile phone today, a computer on the network of your mobile network operator communicates wirelessly to the computer in your mobile phone. A series of commands and responses are traded back between both computers over the network. The combination of the secret credentials stored on your phone, the same credentials stored on the mobile network, and the two computers communicating back and forth with commands and responses is all used in combination to form a security method that eliminated the significant problems of mobile phone cloning which existed in the 1980s and early 1990s at the advent of mobile technology.

TSM uses the same technology to secure a smart phone as a trusted device on networks other than your mobile network. In short, a TSM service provider (for the Google Wallet, First Data provides this service) is responsible for ensuring the credentials of a particular service are stored properly on your mobile phone; then the TSM uses the a network to communicate directly with the mobile phone to ensure the credentials have remained secure over time.

4.4 EMV – Europay, MasterCard, Visa

To combat credit card fraud, a similar system was developed in Europe during the last decade. The system involved including a tiny computer chip into the credit card, and securely storing the credentials of that account within the card. To use this system, the computer on the card needed to be in contact with the computer on a cash register, so the card needed to be inserted into an automatic slot or other device that literally "plugged in" the card into the computer so that the card computer and the cash register computer could trade commands and responses between each other.

In a mobile commerce environment, both GSM and EMV will be employed. While the credentials are stored securely thanks to the TSM, the EMV protocols are used to communicate between the phone and the cash register (or POS device) during a transaction. But, remember, an EMV card needs to be in physical contact with another computer to communicate the required commands and responses. But a smart phone cannot plug in to a cash register – there are simply too many different models of cash registers and too many different models of smart phones to make this feasible. This is where NFC comes in. NFC manages the contactless communication between the smart phone and the POS device, EMV manages the commands and responses between the two devices during a transaction, and, finally, the credentials of a given payment device are held securely with the services of the TSM. That is how all these technologies come together to form a significantly more secure payment environment using mobile commerce, such as the Google Wallet or Isis, than any plastic card.

4.5 Mobile prepaid

While it is unclear whether or not Isis will offer a similar service, Google has announced it will include a Google prepaid card as part of its service. This is extremely interesting from two perspectives:

1. Any card, any type;
2. Breakage, and;
3. Cash reload at POS.

Any payment card, and any other type of payment (such PayPal) will be available through the Google Wallet. Another example of this already exists in a product offered by Starbucks coffee through an iPhone or Android application.

In this example, Starbucks uses a prepaid card that is available for use only in its stores. Once the card account number is stored on the mobile phone that prepaid card, (also known as a stored value card) can be reloaded with any Visa card, MasterCard, American Express card, Discover card, or virtually any other card product in the marketplace today. In addition, other schemes such as PayPal can be used to reload the card. Using this product, a customer can enter their Starbucks application, and reload their account with funds from PayPal, all while standing in line for their morning coffee.

The Google Wallet will work the same way using a new item called the "Google prepaid card", a reloadable stored value card. Note that the Google prepaid card is available as a tender type in any retail store where the Google Wallet is accepted. Also note that the Google prepaid card is branded as MasterCard, allowing for acceptance at any retail store that currently accepts MasterCard's contactless card.

The Google prepaid card is branded as MasterCard, allowing for acceptance at any retail store that currently accepts MasterCard's contactless card.

Figure 11: Starbucks reloadable prepaid

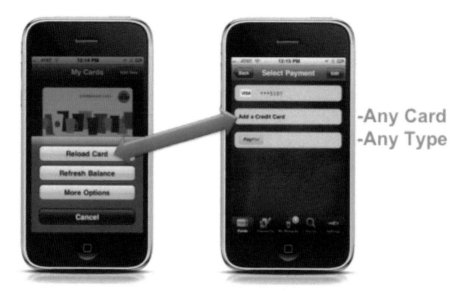

Figure 12: The Google Wallet – image of the Google prepaid card

Figure 13: Accounting 101 refresher

**Assets =
Liabilities +
owner's
equity**

Breakage associated with prepaid cards is a material source of revenue for companies offering these services today. Money that is left unused on a prepaid product is eventually written off the obligations of the company that issued it. Here is how that works: in order to claim the remaining balance on a card that is lost or abandoned, the company cannot book the revenue that it receives at the time that a prepaid card is purchased. For example, when a customer buys a $10 Starbucks prepaid card, Starbucks actually books that $10 amount as a liability, not as revenue. When the customer uses the $10 on the Starbucks store value card that the company considers $10 purchase revenue and at the same time the liability for that $10 is removed from the company's books. But perhaps the customer never spends a full $10, instead spends $9.60. The customer considers the remaining $0.40 on the card insignificant and the customer throws the part away or destroys the card. Starbucks would carry a liability of $0.40 on its books for a period of a year or two, at which point Starbucks will consider that card is lost or inactive, and it will remove that $0.40 liability from its books. But when it removes the $0.40 from its books, the assets of the company increase because liabilities have decreased.

But how much money is that worth?

In 2006, when Starbucks first started accounting for breakage from its prepaid products, it wrote off liabilities in amount of $4.4 million. By the end of fiscal year 2010, that number had ballooned to $31.2 million, which is equivalent to 3.3% of Starbucks' net income for that year. But that number pales against another major retailer: Best Buy. In its fiscal year 2010 annual report, Best Buy showed their breakage on its prepaid card product exceeded $100 million, which is equivalent to 7.6% of Best Buy's net income for the same year.

The opportunity for the greatest market change based on the mobile prepaid card is the simple function of cash reload. Today, a closed-loop gift card at Starbucks can be loaded on to an iPhone or Android phone. Even when in use on the mobile phone, the Starbucks gift card can be reloaded by presenting cash at point of sale. If the prepaid cards of Google Wallet and other mobile wallet companies similarly allow for reload with cash at point of sale, then the population of unbanked people in the United States may have a widely accepted electronic payment method. This is the reason that we project that cash will decline as a tender type of choice as mobile commerce penetration increases (see figure 15, page 32).

Figure 14: Breakage accounts for over $31 million at Starbucks, and $100 million at Best Buy.

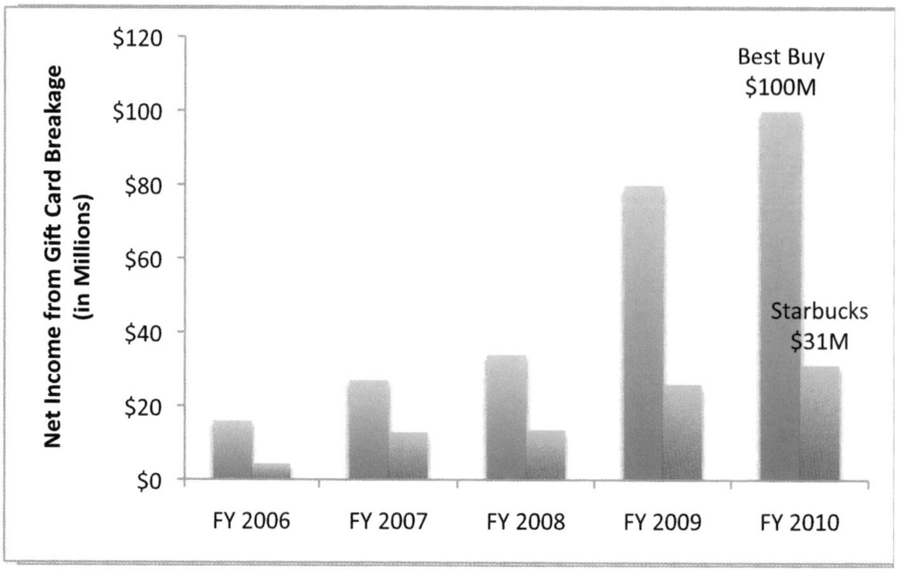

Source: Annual reports of each company.

4.6 Data mining

Data mining is the driver behind targeted advertising. This method attempts to use all available data to try to predict future consumer behavior. Once a customer is profiled to a specific group, a specific shopping pattern, and specific spending habits, that information becomes valuable to a competitor wishing to earn their customers' business or to another retailer interested in maintaining their customers' business.

Never before has a single company been able to see all of the use from all electronic payment types in a given consumer's possession.

While data mining is often employed by individual banks and other companies with access to the data associated with one particular credit card or debit card, and loyalty programs tend to also offer this same type of data, allowing for more targeted consumer advertising, the services contemplated in the global market are unprecedented. Never before has a single company been able to see all of the use from all electronic payment types is a given consumer's possession.

It is not known if Google or Isis will sell this information for the purpose of creating a revenue stream, or perhaps use the information internally to better target various offers to the consumers that use its wallet product. Regardless, data mining has value, and a way will be found to use it for profit; however, sizing the amount of that profit remains to be seen.

Chapter 5

Market forecast

5.1 Phases of development: the timeline

First, models and standards need to be created. At the same time, partnerships among the largest carriers, payments companies, banks, and other industry players need to be formed and understood. Retailers hold the deciding vote, if they choose to use it. Consumers ultimately will be involved only as a function of cost savings and new options available to them presented by retailers.

These systems have to be deployed and adopted. This is a significant expense for retailers, and the notion of multiple companies sharing in the expense of new registers etc. will be significant.

Figure 15: Mobile commerce forecast, 2011 to 2015

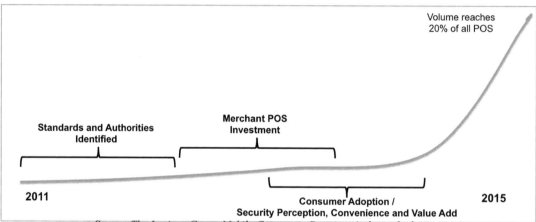

Source: The Luciano Group Mobile Commerce Practice, Author calculations

Finally, consumer adoption needs to achieve critical mass. Given that these products will be free to consumers – or nearly free – the adoption rate is likely to be high if NFC chips begin shipping as standard equipment on most or all phones. [Note – the reason that mobile wallets may not be completely free is because a small fee will be passed on to customers for funds loaded onto a prepaid mobile wallet account from an unassociated credit card.]

Expecting consumers to upgrade their smart phone for the sole reason of enabling payments is unlikely. However, understanding that any GSM phone can easily be upgraded to incorporate an NFC chip, and realizing that the cost of doing that is very low, this too then is an unlikely impediment.

And the final phase, which hopefully will be a long-term effect, is a macro behaviour change on the part of consumers, meaning that they find sufficient convenience, security, and benefits to use the system long-term.

Conclusion

The system that we know as the payments system works reliably and consistently. On the surface, the system is stable, tested, secure, and will reach a total penetration of 63% of all transitions in the United Stated by 2012. However, a new breed of mobile wallet companies are leveraging regulatory pressure and technological advances to create new products, services and business models know as mobile wallets or mobile commerce.

These new products are wisely using the existing payments system for all transaction processing. However, mobile commerce can create new convenient promotional services unlike anything the world has seen before:

- Because a smartphone is a computer and a communications device, it can connect to POS systems and perform transaction functions, creating new retail models and potentially cost efficiencies.
- Because NFC allows for an unlimited command-response dialogue between a smartphone and another device, a customer can 'check-in' to a store and seek discounts and offers applicable to their interests by simply waving their phone at designated point near the entrance of the store, which enables the retailer to interact with a customer while they are in the store. This will allow the retailer to automatically and instantaneously convert a shopper to a buyer.
- A prepaid card on a mobile wallet provides convenience to the customer, interest income to the mobile wallet provider, and a sizeable income from unclaimed funds on the card.
- The potential to expand mobile wallet services to the unbanked population in both developed and undeveloped countries creates a remarkable opportunity to gain mobile commerce market share from the prepaid and stored value tender types.
- The proven security standards of TSM will proactively address the most common concern of consumers: security.
- The retail model of cooperative advertising opens the potential of merchants recouping some of their mobile commerce investment dollars from product manufacturers, allowing for partnerships and cost justification.

The world is watching the Google Wallet and the Isis product because they appear to represent products and services that transcend mere payments or loyalty programs, instead combining technology with new business models, and new services for the consumer. While other types of payment model exist, the information presented in this report represents an indication that the wallet model may indeed emerge as the most significant payment mechanism of the future.

When the Google Wallet formally launched on September 20, 2011, it began testing its services with the Sprint mobile network in the United States in the New York and San Francisco markets. Isis is planning its launch in the Salt Lake City, Utah and Austin, Texas markets also in the United States early in 2012. The results of these tests will determine whether the mobile commerce model will succeed the traditional mobile payments model.

By mid 2012, data from these two tests, and perhaps tests that Amazon and others undertake, will begin to illustrate the mobile commerce/mobile wallet industry that has been shown in this report to be the likely successor to the current payments and loyalty industries.

Based on this analysis, Google Wallet, Isis, and other possible entrants in the emerging mobile commerce industry are in an excellent position to succeed, but only in-market test results over time will prove this hypothesis.

Made in the USA
Charleston, SC
20 February 2012